AQUA

January 20–

Independence is Happiness

✧ Susan B. Anthony ✧

ORCHID

winter

Aquarius

Rebel with a Cause

Objective

INNOVATIVE

REBELLIOUS

INDEPENDENT

Friendly

RULING HOUSE
11
The House of Friendships

AQUARIUS

I never give up on what I believe in

AQUARIUS

Aries

Taurus

Gemini

Cancer

Leo

Virgo

Libra

Scorpio

Sagittarius

Capricorn

Aquarius

Pisces

LET THE STARS LEAD THE WAY